# STOP

## Things You MUST Know Before Trying to Help Someone with Addiction

# STOP

## Things You MUST Know Before Trying to Help Someone with Addiction

**Glenn Rader**

**Maze Publishing**

**Copyright and Disclaimer**

© 2018 by Maze Publishing

The information in this book is not intended or implied to be a substitute for advice from professionals with academic credentials and experience in the field of addiction diagnosis and treatment. The contents of this book represent the author's opinions based on observations made as a participant in a family support group, experience with his successful recovery from addiction, and research in the subject area.

ISBN: 978-1983747144

Printed in the United States of America

Retail ordering: www.amazon.com

General information and questions:

Email: info@mazepublishing.com

"Your assumptions are your windows on the world. Scrub them off every once in a while, or the light won't come in."

**Isaac Asimov**

Special thanks to:

**Karen Bartos**

for her inspiration,
knowledge, and assistance.

# Table of Contents

# Introduction

One of the most significant challenges a person may confront in life is trying to help someone who is struggling with addiction to alcohol or drugs. This represents a unique challenge because many of the actions a person would normally take to help someone in a crisis are not effective in helping someone with an addiction issue. Armed with the wrong assumptions regarding addiction and the pathway to recovery, many people spend years trying to help someone without affecting any change in the person's situation.

People who have success helping a person who is struggling with addiction start from the position that they do not have the necessary tools to be effective. They accept that being a well-intentioned, smart, loving, and otherwise resourceful person is not enough when it comes to helping someone with a physical and psychological disorder — addiction. This is true whether you are dealing with a teenager or an adult with an addiction issue; and whether the person is using marijuana, alcohol, heroin, or another substance.

Another trait of people who have been successful assisting someone with an addiction is they become willing to take actions that seem counterintuitive; actions they would never have considered previously. The confidence to take these actions comes from getting a solid understanding of addiction, recovery, and working with others who have been successful helping an addict. Along with this confidence, they develop an appreciation for the fact that there is no "quick fix" to the situation and that helping someone with an addiction is a process, not an event.

The purpose of STOP is to provide significant information in a short, easy-to-read book that will give you a huge head start on helping someone who is struggling with addiction. It is information that frequently takes people years to learn through trial and error; often at a significant sacrifice from both an emotional and financial standpoint. The information and recommendations in STOP are based on my direct experience working with families and friends of addicts at a major addiction treatment center, personal success with recovery from alcohol and drug addiction, and research on the subject.

The order in which the information in this book is presented is critical. You should read each of the sections of STOP in sequence because the information on addiction, recovery, and misguided beliefs in the early sections is essential to understanding the action steps suggested in the last section. Nothing in this book is conceptually difficult. The most challenging aspect of the information is that you need to be open-minded and willing to embrace a view which may be different from the one you currently have.

# <u>Addiction</u>

It is important to have an informed perspective on addiction because it provides the basis for assisting someone in their recovery. As a starting point, here are two definitions of addiction; one is provided by the field of psychology and the other by the medical field. These short, technical definitions give you a feel for how these important communities view addiction using the terminology of their professions. A practical, working definition of addiction is provided following these technical perspectives.

## American Psychological Association

"Addiction is a chronic disorder with biological, psychological, social, and environmental factors influencing its development and maintenance. About half the risk for addiction is genetic. Genes affect the degree of reward individuals experience when initially using a substance, for example, drugs or engaging in certain behaviors like gambling. Genes also influence the way the body processes alcohol or other drugs. Heightened desire to re-experience use of the substance or behavior, potentially influenced by psychological factors (for example, stress or a history of trauma), social factors (like the use of substances by family and friends), and environmental factors (for example, the accessibility of low cost drugs), can lead to regular use, with chronic use leading to brain changes.

These brain changes include alterations in cortical (pre-frontal cortex) and sub-cortical (limbic system) regions involving the neuro-circuitry of reward, motivation, memory, impulse control, and judgment. This can lead to dramatic increases in cravings for a drug or activity, as well as impairments in the ability to successfully regulate this impulse, despite the knowledge and experience of many consequences related to the addictive behavior."

## American Society of Addiction Medicine

"Addiction is a primary, chronic disease of brain reward, motivation, memory, and related circuitry. Dysfunction in these circuits leads to characteristic biological, psychological, social, and spiritual manifestations. This is reflected in an individual pathologically pursuing reward and/or relief by substance use and other behaviors.

Addiction is characterized by the inability to consistently abstain, impairment in behavioral control, craving, diminished recognition of significant problems with one's behaviors and interpersonal relationships, and a dysfunctional emotional response. Like other chronic diseases, addiction could involve cycles of relapse and remission. Without treatment or engagement in recovery activities, addiction is progressive and can result in disability or premature death."

Looking at both definitions of addiction, it should be apparent that the psychological and medical communities consider addiction to be a serious condition. Words like *genetic*, *chronic disease*, *brain circuitry*, *pathological*, and *progressive* are used to describe addiction. Nowhere in these definitions is there a mention of addiction being caused by someone being an inherently bad person, misbehaving, and this leading to excessive drinking and drugging. Unfortunately, most people start out trying to help an addict with the misinformed perspective that their problem is largely a behavior issue. It is a viewpoint that society shares widely.

## Addiction — Working Definition

To gain a solid understanding of addiction, it is useful to view it from the standpoint of how someone progresses into addiction. This includes the experiences and the physical and emotional changes that occur along the way. The path to addiction can vary from person to person, but there are several elements which appear to be common.

The definition of two terms is required before describing the addiction pathway. These terms are used throughout the book. The first, *mind (mood) altering substance*, means marijuana, alcohol, heroin, cocaine, prescription opiates, or any addictive substance. The second term is *addict.* An addict is someone who continues to use <u>any</u> of the mind-altering substances even though it causes poor decision making and creates negative personal consequences. Traditionally, an addict has been viewed by the public, and portrayed in the media, as someone using "hard" drugs like heroin. The contemporary view, the one used in this book, is that the mind-altering substance a person chooses to use is irrelevant. If they continue to use the substance despite the consequences, they are an addict.

### The Addiction Pathway

1. The Starting Point
2. Initial Exposure
3. Transitional Dependency
4. Delusional Thinking
5. Crossing the Line

### 1. The Starting Point

Before an addict is ever exposed to mood-altering substances, they can have personal characteristics that set them up to be more susceptible than others to the effects. These are the person's genetics and their emotional foundation.

- Genetics — There is significant research to support that an individual's brain chemistry, the physical structure of their brain, liver function, and other physical characteristics can cause them to respond to the effects of alcohol and drugs more intensely than others. It is not unusual for an addict to have a family history that includes relatives who have struggled with addiction.

- Emotional Foundation — Some people are more responsive to the effects of alcohol and drugs because of their emotional needs. Looking back, many addicts describe themselves as having self-esteem issues or "not being comfortable in their own skin." For them, the feel-good effects of mood-altering substances were easily embraced, even though many people were not aware they were using these for relief from their feelings at the time. How people acquire these feelings about themselves vary considerably, ranging from basic experiences as adolescents, like being rejected by a love interest, to living in traumatic, abusive family environments for long periods of time.

It is not a requirement to have the genetic or emotional factors present to become an addict as prolonged exposure to a substance can result in addiction without these factors. However, based on the literature and my discussions with over two hundred recovering addicts about their family histories and emotional experiences, it is highly probable the person you are concerned about has the genetic or emotional elements present.

## 2.  Initial Exposure

Most people experience their first use of mood-altering substances through recreational activities with friends, family members, or coworkers. It could be a school experience with peers, or it might occur as an adult at a family party or work function.

For some people, the occasional use of alcohol or drugs is just another part of socializing and does not result in addiction. For people with a genetic or emotional predisposition, the alcohol or drug represents something quite different; it is a physical and emotional coping mechanism the person unconsciously begins integrating into their day-to-day activities.

## 3.  Transitional Dependency

Following initial exposure, a person can go for years, even decades, making only gradual increases in the quantity and frequency of their use, without knowing they are becoming dependent on the substance. During this period, the substance is making changes to the person's brain circuitry and function.

This includes decision making and behavior surrounding their use of the substance.

To support their addiction, the individual begins hanging out with others, like themselves, and making other changes in their lives to facilitate using alcohol or drugs. Their new "friends" not only provide support for their using, but they also create the illusion that they are a group of people that accept and care about them, fulfilling a basic emotional need.

As the addiction progresses, the addict begins taking advantage of people with whom they have a close relationship (parents, siblings, and friends). They need the help of these people to keep them shielded from the problems related to their addictive behavior and, perhaps, to provide money which can be used to purchase their drug of choice. Lying and dishonesty by the addict become a necessity to keep up the image that things are OK and that they do not have a problem.

## 4. Delusional Thinking and Behavior

When the person reaches this stage in their addiction, the relationship with the substance becomes the most important thing in their lives. This pushes school, family, career, and other responsibilities into the background. The person will use alcohol or drugs despite the consequences, and in contradiction to their most fundamental values, morals, and ethics.

To push the increasing guilt and shame relating to their alcohol and drug use aside, and at the same time justify their continued use, the addict will begin to exhibit delusional thinking and related behavior. At this stage, it is more than making occasional excuses or trying to dance-around the subject of their addiction with clever talk. At this point, the addict behaves as if they mean what they are saying. This includes denying they have a problem, minimizing the seriousness of their situation, and blaming others for their circumstances. Many recovering addicts will tell you they had no idea they were conducting themselves in this extreme and delusional manner. The distorted thinking, rationalization, and related behavior became their new "normal" — their new reality.

## 5. Crossing the Line

Looking back, most recovering addicts will tell you that at some point things seemed to get dramatically worse. It was as if they had "crossed the line." On the other side of that line, the use of alcohol or drugs took on a different level of importance, the same priority as breathing (air).

Research in this area supports that through prolonged use of a substance, it is eventually reclassified by the brain as a survival action. As a survival action, it does not require pondering or assessment before doing it. In other words, the addict's day-to-day functioning requires the substance and they use it without any decision making taking place. The behavior and related negative results are not even considered. Telling the person to stop using is like telling them to stop breathing.

To summarize, addiction is a disease that has a starting point in the genetics and the emotional needs of a person. Through continued use, changes in brain function and emotional dependency will cause an increase in use. This increased use will be accompanied by the development of a support network including new friends and a change in lifestyle. As the disease progresses further, the addict will exhibit delusional thinking and irrational behavior. These are required to support the addiction while ignoring the problems associated with the deteriorating behavior. Eventually, using the substance becomes the number one priority in the person's life, pushing aside all other responsibilities.

## Recovery

Learning about recovery, like addiction, is important for developing an understanding of the actions that are effective in assisting an addict. To begin our discussion on recovery, here is a definition of recovery provided by the U.S. Substance Abuse and Mental Health Services Administration - National Summit on Recovery. A working definition of recovery is provided after the Summit's definition.

### National Summit on Recovery

"Recovery from alcohol and drug problems is a process of change through which an individual achieves abstinence and improved health, wellness, and quality of life."

Summarizing from the Summit's report, it continues:

"There are many pathways to recovery. Although the addict might receive help from others, success will only come if the recovery is self-directed by the addict after they recognize and accept that change is necessary.

Recovery involves achieving a balance of mind, body, and spirit, along with self-redefinition and development of a positive identity. Recovery includes cultivating the ability to look beyond the shame and stigmas associated with addiction.

Recovery can be enhanced by the support of family members, friends, and by rejoining and rebuilding a life in the community. The addict gains hope by interacting with other people in recovery who share their recovery experiences and strength.

Recovery is a reality — it can, will, and does happen for people."

## Recovery — Working Definition

Based on my experience working with successfully recovering addicts, the definition of recovery provided by the Summit is very insightful. The STOP working definition of recovery is a tactical, action-based perspective on recovery that complements the Summit's definition.

The STOP definition focuses on the sequence of key activities that have been observed as critical to successful recovery. As a person trying to help an addict, you are not responsible for performing these functions on behalf of the addict. These are the responsibilities of the addict, the professionals, and the volunteers in the recovery community.

## The Recovery Pathway

1. Surrender
2. Assessment
3. Treatment Selection
4. Detox
5. Abstinence
6. Addiction Education
7. Personal Transformation
8. Long-Term Maintenance

## 1. Surrender

For an addict to seek help for their addiction, and actively participate in the recovery process, they must be self-motivated. To have this occur, the addict must become desperate and reach the decision that the consequences of their addiction outweigh the benefits of using. This is often referred to as reaching the "bottom" in their addiction.

The combination of events that might lead a person to this bottom is different for everyone. Some people reach it through basic incidents like getting into trouble at school or having their spouse threaten to leave them if they do not seek help. Others might experience more serious events such as nearly killing themselves with an overdose or serving prison time for behavior relating to substance abuse. It is not usually a single event, but a series of things over time, which pushes the addict to draw the conclusion that their addiction lifestyle must be abandoned for something better.

The addict does not have to reach this point of desperation entirely on their own. There are actions that a loved one can take, or consciously not take, that can work to "raise the bottom" and move them closer to seeking and participating in treatment. These actions are the subject of the last section of this book.

## 2. Assessment

Once a person has surrendered and is welcoming help for their addiction, they need to have a professional assessment of their situation to determine which treatment options will be the most effective for them. For this assessment, a specialist in addiction treatment should be engaged. These specialists can normally be found at a treatment center or in private practice. If the assessment, or your experience with the addict, points to a possible co-existing psychological disorder like depression, you might also need to engage an independent psychiatrist who has credentials and experience in this area.

It is important to note, if the addict has reached the legal age of adulthood you will not have the authority to force them into an assessment or any aspect of the recovery process. In this case, you would hope the person reaches their point of desperation and becomes willing to proceed with an assessment voluntarily. Even if they agree to an assessment "to get you off their back," it is a move in the right direction.

## 3.  Treatment Selection

The treatment recommended for an individual, as a result of the assessment, may include one or more of the following:

- In-Patient Treatment — These are facilities where a person takes up residence during their treatment. There is a wide range of services offered by the different in-patient treatment centers. The severity of the person's addiction and the availability of funding are factors that influence the person's length of stay at the facility.

- <u>Out-Patient Programs</u> — These are non-residential programs that are normally conducted at a treatment center or similar facility. The out-patient programs do not typically provide medical oversight and several other services.

- <u>Independent Therapy Sessions</u> —These are counseling sessions conducted by therapists in private practice who specialize in addiction treatment. The sessions are performed one-on-one or in small groups.

- <u>Transitional Living Arrangements</u> —These are group-housing facilities for people in recovery that provide a supportive recovery environment (often called half-way or three-quarter houses). These alternative living arrangements can be an excellent option for the person in early recovery, rather than returning home or living on their own.

- <u>Long-Term Support Programs</u> — These are groups that a recovering person can participate in, on an ongoing basis, to help them maintain their new frame-of-mind and lifestyle. Alcoholics Anonymous (AA) and Narcotics Anonymous (NA) are the two well-known 12-Step based programs that fill this important niche. People with substance abuse problems of all types participate in these 12-Step programs.

Regardless of the combination of treatment options selected, the treatment must incorporate five key processes if the person is going to have a chance at successful recovery. These processes represent the remaining components of the pathway to recovery: detoxification, abstinence, addiction education, a personal transformation, and long-term maintenance.

## 4. Detox

Based on the assessment, an addict might require medically supervised withdrawal from the substance (called detoxification or detox) before beginning the other treatment phases. Very frequently, if a person requires detox, it will be the first action taken as part of an in-patient addiction treatment program. A supervised detox might also occur if an addict is taken to a hospital on an emergency basis because of an overdose.

The medical supervision of the detox is required to prevent the addict from experiencing nausea, tremors, insomnia, hallucinations, and convulsions. Based on the nature of the addiction, prescription medicines may be used in the detox process and later in early recovery. This is done to help the addict make a safe, effective transition to a substance-free lifestyle. Any attempt at detox without medical assistance could be fatal.

## 5. **Abstinence**

All effective addiction treatment programs require the addict to stop using mood-altering substances forever, in any form or quantity. Why? Because there is a very high probability that using again will lead them directly back to the addiction. Most recovering addicts who begin using again quickly return to the point at which they left off, and continue getting worse, regardless of how long they have been in recovery.

The reason a person will quickly return to their addiction is twofold. First, the person's genetics do not change in recovery. Their genetic foundation will always be with them and will always respond the same way to addictive substances. Second, the brain's memory of the effects of the substance, especially after long-term abuse, is deep. New routines learned by the addict in recovery can be very effective at keeping these habits in check, but those habits can quickly return through the reintroduction of the substance.

An addict should not participate in any program of recovery that advocates returning to the occasional use of alcohol, or any substance, after a period. This advice is misguided and a very, very risky proposition for both the addict and the people around them who are trying to help.

## 6. Addiction Education

As a part of recovery, the addict needs to learn about the science and psychology of addiction. All quality treatment programs provide this education. Videos, readings, and homework are often used to accomplish this information exchange.

Education related to the technical aspects of addiction is essential to recovery for two reasons. First, when a person enters a recovery program, they have significant guilt and shame about their predicament. They believe that being a bad, irresponsible person with a lack of willpower is the cause of their problem. Learning that their addiction is likely due to other factors is important to free them from the guilt and shame. This new freedom positions them for long-term recovery success. Receiving an education in the science and psychology of addiction also helps them to understand why complete abstinence from alcohol and drugs, and a personal transformation, are important in the recovery equation.

## 7.  Personal Transformation

All the elements of the pathway to recovery play a key role, but the single most important recovery-related process involves the individual experiencing a personal transformation. This transformation involves going from being a delusional, self-centered individual to a person with higher values and new life skills.

The change in the person is accomplished through a sequence of activities involving renewed honesty, personal discovery, one-on-one and group sharing, restoring trust with family and friends, and developing a focus on the well-being of others. As an important part of this process, the person gains insight into their resentments, fears, anger, and other issues, and they develop an understanding of their role in each of these. The process also arms them with tools that can be used on a day-to-day basis to create new relationships with themselves and the people, places, and things around them. The overall result of the transformation is that the person can function with piece-of-mind and without having the coping mechanism of the alcohol or drugs in their life. The addiction is pushed into "remission," while the person enjoys a productive life guided by a new recovery perspective.

All effective in-patient, out-patient, and therapy programs provide assistance to the addict with this transformation. To achieve this, they may use proprietary processes that they develop internally, the tools of Cognitive Behavioral Therapy from professional psychology, and they will often begin introducing the addict to one of the 12-Step programs. You should be very concerned about any treatment program that does not aid with the individual's personal transformation.

## 8. Long-Term Maintenance

Success with recovery is significantly increased by the person staying engaged with a long-term support group. This continued involvement in recovery provides ongoing reinforcement of the principles of recovery, which helps prevent the person from returning to their old values, thinking, and back to the mind-altering substances.

As mentioned previously, the most well-known, long-term support groups are Alcoholics Anonymous (AA) and Narcotics Anonymous (NA). AA and NA are very effective for people who are active in their recovery. The availability of daily AA and NA meetings, a general consistency in practices worldwide, and the very low cost, make AA and NA outstanding long-term recovery support options. Through meetings, presentations, and conventions, a person can interact with other successful recovering people from all walks of life and with a wide range of personal beliefs.

The 12-Step programs of AA and NA are not the only long-term support options for the addict. There are alternatives. These come in the form of groups that are organized by treatment centers or independent therapists in private practice.

As a summary of recovery, a person must become desperate and truly desire recovery before they will seek help voluntarily. After the person commits to recovery, the first steps are to get a professional assessment of their situation and to select treatment options. Next, and as a prerequisite for entering treatment, the person may require medical detox. Upon entering treatment, the first thing the person will be required to do is abstain from using all mood-altering substances. Then, as a part of treatment, they will be provided an education in addiction and begin a personal transformation process to position them for long-term recovery. Last, they will need to join a support group to help ensure their long-term success.

## Misguided Beliefs

As mentioned in the introduction, you can be well-intentioned, loving, smart, and resourceful, but that is not enough when it comes to helping someone with an addiction. To begin with, you need to have an informed, big-picture perspective to understand the actions you can take that will be effective.

There are several common misguided beliefs about addiction and recovery that send people who are trying to help an addict down the wrong path. Despite being told that their assumptions are misdirected, many people will continue operating under the misguided beliefs and then complain that they are not getting any results.

Why do people have such a hard time abandoning their current views and taking on a different perspective? First, it requires them to discard some of their deep-rooted beliefs and feelings about themselves and their relationship with the addict. Second, and to be candid, there are people who are unwilling to embrace change or make the required effort. Try not to be this person. Challenge yourself to be receptive to new ideas. This will be your greatest asset in the effort to help a person with a substance abuse problem.

The purpose of this section of STOP is to provide insight into several of the most significant misguided beliefs on addiction and recovery. Along with each of the misguided beliefs, you are provided an alternative recovery perspective that you can use to guide your thinking and actions. The importance of understanding the messages conveyed in each of these cannot be overemphasized.

### 1. I Caused the Addiction

It is very natural for parents, or someone close to an addict, to believe that they did a poor job of raising the person. Many people feel they are responsible for the addict's circumstances. The guilt and shame from believing you are at fault can be overwhelming.

Holding onto the belief that you caused the person's addiction, you try to make up for the past as a way of fixing the present. You give the addict more of everything and treat them especially nice. You tolerate questionable behavior and "walk on eggshells" to not make them feel bad. Along with this, you spend an incredible amount of time reviewing the past and lamenting over potential actions that might have caused the addiction. While all this is going on, the addict is using your guilt to manipulate you into getting what they want — a primary tool of an addicted person!

Recovery Perspective — Many parents and relatives do a world-class job of raising a child and they still end up with a substance abuse issue. You may have contributed to the person's addiction in some manner. However, the major influences on developing an addiction are most often the person's day-to-day experiences in society beginning with their first day of preschool. This is hard for parents and loved ones to accept, but something you must try to embrace quickly. You need to put aside your feelings of guilt and shame about the past and move forward with objectivity and a focus on the future. If you are doing things today that are adding to the person's self-esteem issues or, on the other extreme, sheltering them from their addictive, problematic behavior, you need to discontinue these actions. The last section of the book provides insight into these areas.

## 2.  The Addict's Problem Is My Problem

Even if you do not have misgivings about your influence on the addict's upbringing, you can still have a dysfunctional relationship with the addict called codependency. In this codependent relationship, you have an unhealthy reliance on the addict's well-being and their approval for your own identity. With this codependent view, you internalize the addiction and the responsibility for recovery as if it were your problem.

In response to the person's addiction, you begin following the addict's every move, monitoring their use, tracking their location, making excuses for them, and covering up their mistakes. You attempt to control the addict's behavior and, at the same time, get their acknowledgment and approval for your efforts. You eventually discover that your ability to directly control anything that the addict is doing is virtually impossible and, since you are doing all the work, they are making no progress toward recovery from the addiction.

Recovery Perspective — This is a good point in the book to invoke a familiar phrase from the recovery community: "You must detach from the addict with love." It may be true that the addiction presents problems for you, but the addict's addiction and related recovery are not your problems.

You need to hold firm to the view that the best outcome for the addict will occur if you stay out of the way and let them take responsibility for their addiction. With you out of the way, the addict will start getting the message that this is their issue to solve and you will be giving them the dignity to try. You must give up the illusion that you can control the addict's behavior and turn your attention to taking care of yourself, both physically and emotionally. Learn what you should do, and what you should not do, to help the addict solve their problem.

### 3. <u>My Poor Little Baby</u>

Many parents and siblings conjure up an image of the addict from the days when the addict was young and "life was good." It is an image of a happy, spirited, free-thinking individual that the addict used to be.

With this image of the addict in mind, you begin drawing on parenting or sibling skills to nurture the naïve, incapable youngster. You believe the addict is a good person at heart; they are just experiencing a tough period and you are going to help by coaching them through it. Treating them like a child, rather than an adult, you try some combination of "spanking," scolding, and rewards to steer them back on the right path.

Recovery Perspective — The best image you can have of an addict is that they can draw their own conclusions, make their own decisions, and take the initiative to help themselves. You will be able to take actions to assist them, but not the actions you would use to nurture a young person.

## 4.  **What Will They Think of Us**

In a very self-centered move, some people who are trying to help an addict will make the entire issue about themselves. This occurs under the belief that what is most important is protecting the image and honor of the family or others around the addict. Operating under this belief, some people direct all their efforts toward protecting this image and sense of honor. This includes hiding the situation from others, making excuses for the addict, continuing to treat the addict as if things are normal, and other misdirected public relations activities.

Recovery Perspective — First, on a practical level, many of the people within the sphere of the addict have observed the addict's actions and are aware there is a problem. Second, it is likely that the people whose opinions you are concerned about have someone in their own family struggling with addiction. They might even be looking at your situation with sympathy and interest rather than the disapproval you might imagine. Third, you are simply not that important. People do not care about your situation as much as you think they do!

It is essential that you put aside any vanity and hold to the belief that addressing the addiction issue transcends any concerns you might have about your family's image and honor.

## 5. They Just Like to Party

It is a commonly held belief that people who abuse alcohol and drugs are just being bad and misbehaving. They are people who like to party too much and are being irresponsible. If they would "get their act together" and drink (use) responsibly, everything would be fine. Unfortunately, this view of addiction is simplistic and could not be further from the truth for people of all ages struggling with addiction.

Recovery Perspective — As described in the sections of STOP on addiction and recovery, addiction is a serious and progressive illness. The alcohol or drug abuse is the symptom — not the cause. It is a physical and emotional obsession, which requires professional attention. All the actions you execute to support the addict must be taken with this in mind.

## 6. Let's Give It Some Time

Along the way, several notions will enter a loved one's mind regarding the addict – "Perhaps they are not that bad off." – "This is probably just a phase like many people go through." – "I did some of this when I was young, and I turned out OK." The conclusion drawn from this thinking is – "Let's give them some time and, perhaps, this will resolve itself." Under this belief, you postpone taking any action.

Recovery Perspective – You might be right about postponing action, but it is a very, very risky proposition considering that you are dealing with a situation that could lead someone to insanity, incarceration, or even death. Addressing someone's addiction is time sensitive. It is a progressive illness. When addressed in early stages, the addict will have an improved chance of responding to treatment and long-term recovery. You must be careful you are not in denial about the addict's situation and making excuses for not moving forward with taking action.

## 7. They Are Falling Behind Their Peers

As a part of the addiction recovery effort, it is common for people to try to keep their loved one on track in all aspects of their life. At the same time the addict is struggling with addiction, and perhaps trying to be active in treatment, the people in their life are trying to prevent them from falling behind their peers at school, work, or in relationships. For example, after having left college because of substance abuse issues, it is not uncommon for parents to send a young person back to college before their substance abuse has been addressed. This action is driven by an idealistic vision of the perfect family, its perfect members, and the perfect path to success in life.

Recovery Perspective — Addressing the individual's addiction should be the number one priority. You, and the addict, should approach the situation from the standpoint that a healthy physical and mental foundation is a prerequisite to success in all other areas of life. The person might lose a few steps in the short-term while addressing their addiction. However, with a clear head and a new view of themselves and the people around them, their long-term success will certainly be greater than if they had continued their destructive, addictive lifestyle.

## 8.  I Know What I Need to Do

When people become convinced that their loved one has a substance abuse problem, many will jump right in to solve the problem. Very often, there is no thought of getting professional guidance before acting.

Using your best intentions and skills, you put forth a plan to "whip the addict into shape". You sit the addict down and have a talk that includes strong, emotional warnings about the risks of addiction and the dismal future that goes along with it. This talk is followed by giving the addict some helpful suggestions on what they should do to reduce their abuse of the substance. This might even include some offers of rewards if they can "straighten up." In the end, what you are doing is the same as trying to treat cancer with chicken soup and aspirin — ineffective home remedies.

Recovery Perspective — You should start from the position that you do not have the tools to help someone with an addiction. You need to become a student of addiction, recovery, and the things that will help the addict and you. You are the student here, not the teacher.

## 9.  I Am Failing at Helping — I Must Try Harder

Another belief that people hold is that they know what to do to help the addict change, but they are just doing a poor job at executing the task. For example, you have been stopping over at the addict's house to bring them food and give them support, but this does not seem to be helping. Therefore, you conclude you need to stop over more often, do a few more things for them while you are there, and maybe that will have an impact.

What it boils down to is you are doing a fantastic job — you are just doing a fantastic job at the wrong things. This is not a common cold someone is getting over where a little kindness and more attention on your part will help them get through a tough time. What you are doing may seem intuitive, but it is not productive.

Recovery Perspective — The number of actions you have available to help an addict are very limited, but if executed effectively you can have a significant impact. What you must do is target your efforts at doing a great job at the right things. Being a kind, concerned person is very important, but your actions must be grounded in the experience of people who have succeeded and failed in trying to help someone with an addiction. The purpose of STOP is to bring this information to you in an accelerated manner.

## 10. If I Don't Help Them — They Will Get Worse

One of the principles you were introduced to under the subject of recovery is that the individual must experience the consequences of their addiction as motivation for surrendering and getting into treatment. You might be having trouble buying into this premise because you feel if you do not help them with their problem, they will feel worse and use even more.

As an example, because your son is staying out late and getting "high," he is not getting up on time and is frequently late for his summer job. He needs this job to earn money for college next year. You believe if he loses the job, he will slip even further into the addiction because he will feel bad about losing the job. Further, you are concerned he will have more time to use his substance of choice.

Your response to the situation is to start waking your son up every day to ensure that he gets to work. Now the addict has the best of both worlds. He gets to go out at night and get "high", and he keeps his summer job because someone is waking him up. The result is that he is being shielded from the problems associated with the addiction and the disease continues to progress.

Recovery Perspective — In the example, if your son oversleeps, loses his job, and you do not provide additional funds for college, this just might move him toward accepting help for the addiction. You should hold true to the belief that compensating for the addict's problems is not supporting them in recovery.

## 11. The Safest Place for Them Is My Home

It would seem logical if you give the practicing addict a place under your roof, meals, and lodging, they are going to have the best chance of getting things straightened out. This feeling is particularly strong when it comes to supporting a young adult. With them in your home, you can keep an eye on them, provide the essentials, and help them to make course corrections in their decision making when required.

Recovery Perspective — The one thing an active addict needs most, to allow them to practice their addiction without disruption, is a roof over their head, a place to sleep, and food to eat. With this, the addict can continue with the delusional thinking that everything is OK and that no change on their part is required. They will "milk" the situation as long as possible, while the addiction continues to grow, and you continue to believe you are helping.

Providing a place to live and the essentials is a mistake unless the person is active in a program of recovery and they are meeting all the other requirements of the household. As counterintuitive as it might seem, this is even true for an 18-year-old son or daughter.

## 12. **We Must Sacrifice Everything**

The last misguided belief relates to the amount of personal sacrifice you feel you must make in the process of trying to help an addict. It is not uncommon for people trying to help an addict to believe that they need to pour all their available resources into the addiction problem. This includes physical, emotional, and financial resources. Holding onto this belief, people will empty their savings accounts, mortgage their homes, or otherwise sacrifice their own physical and emotional well-being to help the addict.

Recovery Perspective — Making a physical, emotional, or financial investment in the situation will likely be required. How far you care to go in this regard is a very personal decision. If you are spending everything you have trying to address the issue, you are probably going about it the wrong way. You are likely sacrificing your well-being by providing emotional and financial "cushions" and "safety nets" for the addict. In turn, the addict is not truly experiencing the gravity of their situation. You have a right to a good life, including a safe place to live, peace of mind, and your retirement savings. Some addicts are simply incapable of recovery and you do not have to go down with a sinking ship.

## How to Help the Addict

This section represents the heart of STOP. On the following pages, you are provided the action steps that can be effective in helping someone struggling with addiction. First, you are introduced to your general responsibilities. This is followed by a description of the actions that support each of the responsibilities.

All of the action steps presented in this section are suggestions. Therefore, you should develop a relationship with the professionals and volunteers in your local addiction recovery community for idea sharing and to validate actions you might be considering. The friendship, information, and peace of mind that you can get from these people are remarkable.

The following defines what "helping" means when it comes to the subject of assisting someone with an addiction.

## Responsibilities

1. Get outside support for yourself from the addiction recovery community.

2. Establish a recovery relationship with the addict.

3. Do not enable the addiction by shielding the person from the consequences of their addictive behavior.

4. Set boundaries with the addict to prevent unacceptable behavior and to protect your well-being.

5. Create a supportive, recovery-oriented environment for the addict.

6. Conduct a formal intervention with the addict if you believe it is appropriate.

7. Secure your personal property and other assets from abuse by the addict.

8. Continue to perform your responsibilities whether or not the addict is in recovery.

Solid execution of these recovery-oriented

responsibilities will encourage the addict to pursue treatment and to participate in a long-term recovery process. You will also benefit from sticking to these responsibilities because you will have the best opportunity for enjoying a good quality of life, whether they seek recovery or not.

You should not be discouraged by what might appear to be a formidable list of responsibilities. There is some work involved, but these responsibilities, and the related action steps, are very manageable. The total amount of effort and time, and the emotional and economic impact on you, will be far less than if you embark on a haphazard journey based on gut feeling, intuition, and incorrect assumptions. There is no guarantee any of this will work, but your chances of success are significantly better if you take this perspective on "helping."

Regarding the order in which the responsibilities are presented, this is a suggested sequence of execution. The dynamics of your situation, and where you are in the process with the addict, could dictate a different order. Also, you will likely be addressing several of these at the same time. Regardless, the first thing you should do is get outside support because this is where you will get guidance and wisdom throughout the process.

# Action Steps

### Responsibility #1

### Get outside support for yourself from the addiction recovery community.

It should be apparent at this point in the book that getting professional and volunteer community support is essential. There are four types of information and support you should seek out:

1.  A background in addiction and recovery,

2.  The first-hand experience of others in your situation,

3.  Assistance with issues you might have like anger, guilt and trust, and

4.  Information for the addict on recovery resources and treatment options.

There are several places you can go for these:

Addiction Treatment Centers — These are centers that offer assessment, detox, in-patient and out-patient treatment, and other services to support recovery. Along with these services, they often provide support for family members and friends of addicts in all four of the above areas. If not, they can point you in the right direction.

<u>Community Service Organizations</u> — These are state, regional, or city organizations that have been established in your area to assist people who are struggling with addiction, as well as their families and friends. Again, if they do not provide one or more of the support services, they can usually suggest where you can find these.

<u>Addiction Therapists</u> — These independent therapists specialize in addiction treatment for the addict and support for family members and friends. Like the treatment centers, a therapist may provide support in one or more of the four areas. It is important that the therapist has, and can demonstrate, specific credentials and expertise in addiction counseling and treatment.

<u>12-Step Support Groups</u> — In addition to the other support resources you engage, you should join one of the 12-Step based support groups for families and friends. Like Alcoholics Anonymous (AA) and Narcotics Anonymous (NA) for the addict, the most extensive support network for loved ones of an addict is their counterpart organizations Al-Anon and Nar-Anon. These are one of the best resources you can access

for support in areas #2 and #3.

Comparable to the personal transformation process the addict must experience, these 12-Step support groups take the family members and friends through their own personal transformation. Through this process, you develop insight into your resentments, fears, anger, and other issues. Most people emerge from this process with an entirely different perspective on the situation and an invaluable set of relationship tools that significantly improve their ability to work with the addict.

The one thing that all of these support resources have in common is that they usually involve face-to-face interaction with others. The transformation observed in family members and friends who participate with others in the same type of situation is incredible. When surrounded by people in similar circumstances, the fear begins to leave their faces and they become capable of dealing with situations with a level of confidence and a calm demeanor that they would not have dreamed possible.

What about the internet as a source of information? It is a great resource, but it is not effective as a primary resource. Another caution! The last place you should look for help is from family members and friends. Without specific background and experience with addiction and recovery, their support will be emotional, reactive, and most often based on misguided beliefs.

What about providing information to the addict on recovery resources and treatment options? It is very effective for you to accumulate and present various recovery resources and options to the addict for addiction treatment. This should be done after you have established a recovery-oriented relationship with the addict; at appropriate points in your discussions when the addict is not "high" and when the nature of the conversation is cordial.

## Responsibility #2

### Establish a recovery relationship with the addict.

The actions falling under this area of responsibility are specifically designed to position you to have a productive, recovery-oriented relationship with the addict. The nature of this relationship is important because the way the addict perceives you and the consistency and tone of your interactions will greatly influence your success with them.

- Relationship Foundation — Drawing on material from previous sections of the book, there is some key information that you should keep in mind as you establish this relationship:

1. The person is physically sick and not thinking clearly,

2. They will embrace change by experiencing the results of their addictive behavior,

3. Recovery is a process that takes time,

4. You must put aside the guilt and shame for what you think you might have contributed to the situation, and

5. You must detach emotionally from their issue. Give up trying to control things. Form a relationship that is grounded in objective, fact-based interactions.

- Guiding Principle — As you consider how you will interact with the addict and which actions you are going to take, a useful guiding principle is to ask yourself the following question: "Do I want the addict to get better or do I want them to like me?" It would be great to achieve both goals. However, too many errors are made by people who unconsciously focus on not making the addict displeased with them. They make this their primary goal and the basis for decision making. Why do people do this? Because it is human nature to want the person to like you, even if they have an addiction issue. Unfortunately, making this your primary goal is the easy way out. It is a short-term solution, which comes at a significant long-term cost to the addict and you.

- <u>Expectations of Yourself</u> — All of your interactions with the addict should be compassionate, without anger, judgment, or blame and with a willingness to listen. You should behave this way even if you must fake it until you get good at it (or as they say in the recovery support community — "Fake it until you make it!"). Adhering to this relationship style will get you significantly more mileage with the addict than if you are a frantic, demanding, accusing, and controlling individual. A good example of the image you want to project is how you might expect a doctor or professional therapist to behave with you, friendly and compassionate, but also objective and well-informed.

- <u>Expectations of the Addict</u> — You should expect the addict to conduct themselves respectfully in all aspects of your relationship. There should be no tolerance for verbal or physical tirades, emotional outbursts, or incoherent behavior on their part. This includes communications done in-person, over the phone, in emails, or through text messages. If the addict is behaving in this manner, they are usually expressing denial, projecting blame, rationalizing their use, or minimizing their addiction. It is likely that they are not even aware they are behaving in this manner, but that does not mean that you must put up with it. When this type of behavior occurs, a boundary is needed between you and them regarding your expectations in the relationship. Setting boundaries is the subject of Responsibility #4.

- <u>The Timing of Interactions</u> — Your interactions with the addict should take place, whenever possible, when they are sober — not "high." Speaking with someone when they are under the influence of a substance is a waste of time for everyone involved. If the person engages you when they are using, unless it is an emergency, you should let them know that you would be glad to discuss the subject with them when they are not using, then disengage.

- <u>"The Conversation"</u> — As soon as you feel you have enough information and support, you should meet with the addict to have a conversation about your recovery relationship with them. For this dialogue, it is essential that you draw on all of the relationship principles and that you prepare, in advance, what you are going to say and the next actions you are willing to take. This is not an intervention in a conventional sense. The purpose of the conversation is to express your concerns, offer your support in their recovery, and to communicate responsibilities. To assist you, one of your outside resources can be accessed to help design the message. Here is a short example of the information that you might share during this conversation.

---------------

"Jim, we love you very much, but we are concerned about you. You have changed. Your personality and behaviors are not those of the person we knew. We believe substance abuse, and the issues underlying the abuse, are presenting problems for you. We are not angry. It is not your fault, but it is something that you need to address.

We are here to let you know that we will support you in getting help for the addiction in any way we can, but we will not do things for you that support the addiction in any way. You are responsible for all aspects of your day-to-day life and for addressing the results of any poor behavior relating to the addiction.

If you are willing to accept help, we are willing to start the process today."

---

You might get a nice surprise, if they take you up on your offer. More likely, their response will come in the form of denial, anger, or blame, followed by declining your offer. Do not be discouraged! What you will have accomplished, at a minimum, is putting the person on notice about the nature of your relationship going forward. You will also get the satisfaction of knowing you are being proactive and trying to do everything you can.

- <u>Emergency Situations</u> — It is prudent for you to consider, in advance, what you will do if the addict is acting dangerously. Examples of this include physical acts against you and others, suicide threats, robbery, or property destruction. These are all situations where engaging someone from the law enforcement or emergency medical communities would be justified and appropriate. Yet, you might hesitate to act because you fear your actions will result in a police record and long-term issues for the addict. The problem with not taking the action, which is normal and customary for such behavior, is that you are, in a sense, condoning the behavior.

Several of the relationship principles you learned about in this section can be effective with everyone, not just the addict. This includes your relationships with outside support people, your spouse or significant other, family members, and friends. Like interaction with the addict, you will make a lot more progress with everyone if you are calm, cool, and collected, rather than frantic, emotional, and reactive.

## Responsibility #3

**Do not enable the addiction by shielding the person from the consequences of their addictive behavior.**

The actions described in this section are different from the other areas because this section focuses on things that you should <u>not</u> do. By avoiding certain actions, you can have an impact on the addict's awareness of their addiction and the seriousness of their situation.

As the addiction progresses, the addict's ability to function normally day-to-day, to manage the results of their poor behavior, and to maintain healthy relationships with people becomes more and more difficult. You might expect with the increasing turmoil in their lives that the addict would begin to question the wisdom of their ways and start considering that a change might be in order. Then, something gets in their way of drawing this conclusion — YOU!

In the interest of being helpful, you step in and begin taking care of their problems, which shields them from the results of their addictive behavior. Along with this "help," you continue to issue warnings to the addict about the problems their addiction is creating and their eventual demise. In the end, you find your words are not making a difference. Why? Because, as it has been put by addicts in recovery, "Warning me about the fire was not enough. I needed to feel the heat!" They are not getting a chance to feel the heat because your actions are putting out the fire.

This dysfunctional help by people is called enabling the addict or enabling the addiction. Enabling is the process of helping them solve their addiction-related problems while thinking that you are helping them out of their addiction. Instead, you are deferring their reality, keeping them dependent on you, preventing them from maturing, and fostering their addiction.

Why do people have such a hard time avoiding the "rescuer/fixer" role? It can be explained, in large part, by their misunderstanding of addiction and recovery, and by operating under the misguided beliefs previously illustrated. If you examine enabling at a very basic level, helping someone in troubled times is much easier and more rewarding to you than watching them falter and struggle. In a sense, the addict takes the substance for instant relief for their addiction, and you take care of the addict's problems as a form of instant relief from your obsession — THEM! As you continue to perform these enabling actions, the addict is concluding that things are not that bad and the disease keeps progressing.

When you stop enabling the addiction, it can represent a real turning point in your relationship with the addict and the impact you are having on their situation. Avoiding enabling actions is an art, not a science, and it will often come in small steps. Here are several examples of enabling.

### Enabling Examples

- Finishing their household responsibilities including homework, cleaning, paying bills, and shopping,

- Planning the addict's activities for them to prevent them from failing at future obligations,

- Paying their monthly mortgage or rent, car payments or leases, auto insurance, utilities, and other bills,

- Allowing the person to live in your home when

they are not meeting the requirements of living there,

- Giving the addict cash or cash equivalents (things they can turn into cash like gas cards),

- Paying for attorneys, bailing them out of jail, and other support activities associated with legal problems,

- Making excuses, lying, and hiding things from people at their school, work, and from family and friends,

- Blaming other people, places, and things for causing the behavior of the addict,

- Tolerating bad behavior in the form of verbal or physical abuse, theft, and damage to your property,

- Avoiding expressing your feelings with the addict, and

- Not taking care of yourself by making the addict's needs a priority over your own.

You can imagine how someone who is dependent on a substance, and operating with increasing delusional thinking, could conclude that "I don't have a problem" if people are doing the things demonstrated in these enabling examples. The addict might believe there is a fire, but they are not feeling the heat. It is also worth pointing out that any one of your actions involving providing cash, cash equivalents, or similar funding is particularly enabling. With additional cash in hand, or by freeing up their available cash by paying for things, they are in a better position to acquire more of their substance of choice.

You might elect to perform an enabling action under one condition, if it will reinforce the recovery relationship with the addict. This is accomplished by letting the person know you are helping them with the situation this one time, but that you will never do it again. This is called setting a boundary, which is the subject of the next section.

Overall, the best thing you can do is maintain an active awareness of potential enabling actions by asking the question: "Is what I am doing supporting some aspect of the person's addictive behavior?" Then, as reinforcement for your decision, try drawing on your recovery relationship guiding principle: "Do I want the addict to get better or do I want them to like me?"

## What about the community enablers?

Family members, friends, significant others, and coworkers of the addict, just about anyone, can take on the role of enabler. This is referred to as community enabling.

Operating without a background in addiction or recovery, and being guided by one or more of the misguided beliefs, these people will usually turn to some form of enabling to assist the addict. Further, if they are one step removed from the addict, both physically and emotionally, they might even knowingly do something that is enabling with the confidence that they can walk away from the situation if things get worse.

If you want to be proactive concerning community enabling, you should focus your efforts on the following people:

1. If the addict is living in your home, everyone else who resides there,

2. Individuals outside of the home who have already started enabling the addict; someone you believe the addict may be taking advantage of, and

3. People who come to you expressing concern about the addict.

There are three actions that you should consider taking with respect to these people:

1.  Have a conversation with them to convey key information regarding the situation,

2.  Invite the person to participate with you in one or more of your support groups, and

3.  Give them a copy of this book to read. STOP was specifically written to help you and others in the sphere of the addict.

If they do not respond to any of your suggestions, discontinue trying to influence or control their actions and lead by your example. Relative to the conversation suggested in #1, it might go something like this:

———————————

"As you may or may not be aware, Jim is having some challenges with substance abuse. Addiction behaves like a progressive disease and it is affecting Jim's thinking and actions. I am getting professional advice and assistance with all aspects of the situation. There is some information that I would like to share with you.

Regarding your interactions with Jim, always try to be compassionate, calm, and understanding, but do not engage with him when he is under the influence of alcohol or drugs and being unreasonable with you. Simply end the conversation and let him know that you would be glad to discuss things when he is not using and when the dialogue can be cordial. If he is ever threatening to you or himself (suicide), call the police.

Relative to assisting Jim, in any way, it is very important for you to consider the following. When a person struggling with addiction begins experiencing issues in their life due to the addiction, they will come looking for help from others. NOT help with the addiction, but with the things in their life that are slipping because of the addiction. This will include soliciting people for money that the addict will ultimately use to purchase alcohol or drugs. If you provide Jim with help of this kind, he will not be experiencing the consequences of his addiction, he will not seek treatment, and the disease will continue to progress.

Here are some examples of things you might do, with love and good intent, which could contribute to Jim's addiction. (Provide them several examples from the list on pages 53 and 54.) If Jim asks you for assistance with any of these types of things, please consider the potential ramifications of meeting his request. Remember, you have no obligation to solve his problems. If you ever want to talk about any action you are considering with Jim, please get in touch with me."

_____

Some of the people you have this conversation with might be in denial about the addict's situation or feel they know more than you do about what should be done. Do not be concerned about their reaction. At a minimum, you will get the satisfaction of knowing you are doing everything you can about the situation by having the discussion with them. Also, the person could tell the addict about your conversation. This might be followed by a confrontation between you and the addict. If this occurs, use your recovery relationship tools and approach the situation with an objective, calm, matter-of-fact approach.

### Responsibility #4

**Set boundaries with the addict to prevent unacceptable behavior and to protect your well-being.**

The previous section focused on actions that you should not take; actions that might shield the addict from their addictive behavior. Another very effective tool is called setting boundaries. What does a boundary look like? Here is an example:

————————————

"If you are disrespectful to your father or me, we will take away your cell phone and take you off the service plan."

————————————

Setting boundaries with the addict involves defining behavior that is unacceptable to you, your family, or society, then implementing consequences if the addict chooses to violate the boundary. Boundaries are not directly set to force the person to seek treatment for their addiction. Boundaries are set to prevent the addict's behavior from affecting your emotional well-being and physical surroundings. By having boundaries set with them, and by them experiencing a negative outcome if they violate a boundary, the hope is that the addict will become more aware of the serious nature of their circumstances.

The phrase, "They choose to violate the boundary.", is important to note because the addict must view the consequence as being a direct result of their behavior. For example, if an addicted young adult who is living in your house violates a boundary which results in them having to move out of your home, they are said to have "made a choice" to move out of your home — you didn't throw them out. As part of setting a boundary, you should let them know the outcome of violating the boundary is their choice.

Regarding the consequence part of the boundary, a consequence can be in the form of an action that you take (for example, taking your son's cell phone away if they are disrespectful to you), or in the form of something you stop doing (for example, not visiting your sister's home if she has been drinking).

Some people have trouble setting boundaries for a couple of reasons. First, setting a boundary confronts you with some of your own deepest, misguided beliefs. Second, when you try to establish a boundary or implement the consequence for a violated boundary, you will usually get pushback from the addict. You should not let this pushback deter you from moving forward.

Effective boundaries have several important characteristics. As you define your boundary conditions and the related consequences, keep the following characteristics in mind:

### Boundary Characteristics

- Controllable — You must have direct control over the conditions and consequences you are going to establish with the addict. For example: "If you get high with your friends, you will not be allowed to hang out with them." will not work. How can you monitor when they are getting "high" or hanging out with their friends?

- Specific — The boundary must be well defined. For example: "If we come to visit and we even think you have been drinking (condition), we are going to leave (consequence)." Both are specific.

- Measurable — If the boundary involves quantities, they must be measurable. For example: "If you continually come home late, we will move your curfew up by one hour." How will you measure "continually" in this context?

- Reasonable — If a condition or consequence is unreasonable, it will usually fail in all respects. For example: "If you look at us in a funny way, we will not talk to you for five years." This is not a reasonable condition or consequence.

- Meaningful — The boundary needs to be meaningful in all respects. For example: "If you continue decorating your bedroom with beer advertising posters, we will no longer invite you to the movies with us." Neither the condition nor consequence are very meaningful.

- <u>A Stick Not a Carrot</u> — The boundary needs to be set for preventing unacceptable behavior, not for rewarding good behavior. For example: "If you stop using marijuana, we will get you a new car." This would not be a good idea! Stopping the use of marijuana is not treating the addiction.

All actions you establish for violated boundaries must be something that you can follow through with if the conditions surrounding the boundary are breached. Setting boundaries and then not following through, or letting the person negotiate or change the boundary, is a major mistake in the context of trying to help an addict. This will seriously undermine your efforts going forward.

What if you set a boundary and then realize that it does not meet one or more of the good boundary characteristics? In this instance, you should not ignore it. You should adjust the boundary or eliminate it and then have a discussion with the addict about the change. The goal should be to set good boundaries in the first place. A lot of redefinition and change is as bad as not holding the addict accountable for adhering to well-defined boundaries.

## The Flow of Cash

The best opportunities you will have for setting

boundaries are when you control the funding for a person's basic needs and lifestyle. A good example of this is when you have someone, a young person or adult, living at your residence. In addition to giving them a place to stay, you might be providing food, an allowance, clothing, a car, car insurance, college tuition, a cell phone, or internet service. All these items require an outlay of cash on your part and represent good opportunities to create negative outcomes for inappropriate, addictive behavior.

If the addict is living outside of your home, you will still find that "cash is king" relative to setting boundaries. However, the amount of control you will have over the boundary conditions, and the actions available to you, will be more limited in scope. The need for money from an addict living outside of your home will often come in the form of mortgage payments, rent, food, clothing, transportation, or funding for legal problems. In the end, if they do not get into recovery, the money will ultimately be used to purchase alcohol or drugs.

## Your Personal Time

Next to cash, the best opportunity to set a boundary involves your personal time. It is not unusual to find people who are enabling and not setting good boundaries, driving the addict around town, going grocery shopping for them, cleaning their house, calling their work and making excuses for absences, or spending hours on the phone listening to them. You have the right to use your time for your activities, interests, and pursuits. Make sure that you are setting healthy boundaries regarding your time because, if you do not, the delusional addict will continue to conclude that help is always available and that everything is OK.

## I Can't Do That!

A real challenge for people is setting a boundary where the appropriate consequence seems much too severe to the boundary setter; something they cannot imagine doing. These situations usually occur when the nature of the consequence challenges their most fundamental beliefs as a parent, sibling, or loved one. To demonstrate, here are three examples that come up frequently in family support groups.

The first one relates to putting someone, usually a young adult, out of your home because of a boundary violation. Putting someone out of your home, with nowhere to stay, and perhaps without a job or source of income, is a very hard thing for people to do. Yet, there are people who do just that, with great success. Why? It is the best option for the addict's well-being and long-term welfare.

The second difficult area that comes up frequently is deciding whether to support someone when they have legal problems. The challenge here is that if you are asked to provide funding for an attorney or bail, and you do not provide it, the person might incur a felony charge or jail time. However, the level of their addiction and continued deteriorating behavior might dictate the need for legal outcomes at this level to help them reach their point of desperation.

Last, and as noted under Responsibility #2, there are emergency situations in which calling the police or emergency medical services (EMS) would be the appropriate consequence for a certain type of addictive behavior. However, some people will hesitate because of the potential ramifications to the person. You would not hesitate for a minute to call the police if a stranger was threatening you or committing an act of vandalism, theft, or physical abuse. Nevertheless, with someone you know, you hesitate. You must be prepared for this type of situation to come up when you are trying to help an addict. Setting a boundary that includes calling the police or EMS may be the best option.

Here are several examples of addictive behavior for which people set boundaries:

## Setting Boundaries
## Examples of Addictive Behavior

- <u>Substance Abuse</u> — Alcohol or drug related activity inside the home or with the family outside of the home. This includes being "high" around you, the presence of substances and paraphernalia, and associating with addicted friends in your company.

- <u>Inappropriate Communications</u> — Yelling, vulgar language, insults, sarcasm, or being unresponsive by giving you the silent treatment.

- <u>Deception</u> — Lying, cheating, making excuses, blaming, or manipulation.

- <u>Physical Abuse</u> — Threats or acts of violence and doing bodily harm.

- <u>Time Abuse</u> — Abuse of your personal time for transportation, shopping, or meeting with outside parties regarding issues that arise. Constantly barraging you with lengthy, substance-induced text messages, emails, or phone calls.

- <u>Property Damage</u> — Destruction of the home, its

contents, automobiles, and other assets.

- <u>Theft</u> — Stealing cash, jewelry, and other property.

- <u>Default on Obligations</u> — Not meeting commitments and requirements relating to home chores, curfews, school, or work.

- <u>Cash Abuse</u> — Requests for cash to fund obligations that cannot be met such as rent, car payments, or credit card debt.

- <u>Illegal Activity</u> – Driving under the influence, dealing drugs, and other issues with law enforcement and the court system.

- <u>Not Participating in Recovery</u> — If they are living in your home and they have recently entered an addiction recovery process, you can set a boundary around them participating in recovery as a condition of living in your home.

The following are examples of consequences used as a part of setting a boundary:

## Setting Boundaries
## Examples of Consequences

- <u>Cash Support</u> — Not spending money on their behalf for an allowance, gas, clothing, car insurance, college expenses, cell phone, internet service, rent, utilities, or other items.

- <u>Personal Property</u> — Not allowing access to your home, your cars, or anything that they currently use that belongs to you.

- <u>Communications</u> — Not participating in communications with them including in-person dialogue, phone calls, emails, or text messages.

- <u>Your Time</u> — Not driving them around or otherwise making yourself available for various tasks requiring your time.

- <u>Family Events</u> — Not inviting them to holiday celebrations, family dinners, or other events.

- <u>Restrictions</u> — Changing their curfew, reducing the amount of time they are permitted to use their computer, or other restrictions.

- <u>Legal Support</u> — Not funding attorneys, bail, or court-related expenses.

Here are a few examples of setting boundaries around addictive behavior (the condition) combined with what will occur if they do not meet the condition (the consequence):

## Boundary Examples
## Conditions and Consequences

- "There will be zero tolerance for you having alcohol or drugs in this house. That means you cannot be high around us or have alcohol, drugs, or drug-using supplies on our property. If you do, it means that you have chosen not to live in our home and you will be required to pack up and move out with no financial support from us."

- "We expect you to be respectful with us and others in the household at all times. This includes face-to-face conversations, on the phone, emails, and text messages. If you choose not to be respectful, we will take away your car and car insurance."

- "If you threaten suicide, we will call the police."

- "We will not speak with you when you have been drinking."

- "If you damage our home or any of its contents, you will not be permitted to come into our home again."

- "We are hiring an attorney and paying your bail to support you this one time, and one time only. We will never provide this support again."

- And under the assumption that a person has entered a recovery process — "As a condition of living in our home, you must actively participate in a program of recovery as recommended to you by your treatment program."

If you feel that you need some guidance, you can always discuss the boundaries you are considering with someone from your support group. Also, before you communicate the boundary to the addict, put it down in writing. Having it in writing will help ensure that it makes sense and flows logically. Keeping a copy of the boundary in writing is also a great backup if one of the parties involved has a "memory issue." Last, communicate the boundary to the addict when they are sober.

## Responsibility #5

### Create a supportive, recovery-oriented environment for the addict.

One of the first recommendations made to all recovering addicts in a treatment program is to avoid people, places, and things that represent "triggers" for their addiction. This would include avoiding situations that involve the use of mind-altering substances, but also people, places, and things that present unusual emotional challenges to the addict.

Eventually, when the recovering person has developed a solid sobriety toolkit and gained some experience with living a sober life, they will be able to navigate all the normal day-to-day situations. Until then, and while the person is in early recovery, following the advice of the recovery community is essential for the addict — "Avoid wet faces and wet places."

As a concerned person, one of the direct contributions you can make to help an addict is doing whatever you can to create a supportive, recovery-oriented environment for the addict. You can accomplish this by making the environment you control free of mind-altering substances and by reducing stressful situations. The focus of this section of STOP is to provide several important actions that you can take toward realizing these goals.

## In Your Home

If you have someone struggling with addiction living in your home, or visiting frequently, the physical presence of, and <u>your</u> use of, mind-altering substances around them should be eliminated 100%. Taking this action means you discontinue the use of, and remove from your home, alcohol, marijuana, and all other substances. Along with this, you should remove all pipes, rolling papers, and drug-related paraphernalia. If you have prescription medicines in the home, these should be secured under lock and key.

You would think that removing the presence and use of mind-altering substances from your home, for the benefit of someone you love, would be an easy decision. Surprisingly, some people find it difficult. Here are the four major reasons/excuses why people are not willing to take this important action.

First, some people will continue using alcohol in their home when they have an addict living with them who is addicted to, for example, heroin. This is done under the belief that since the substances are not the same, it will not present a problem. The correct perspective is that all mind-altering substances must be treated as being detrimental to the addict, not just their immediate drug of choice. The presence and use of alcohol in front of a heroin addict are the same as the presence and use of heroin in front of a heroin addict.

The second reason that people will not eliminate all mind-altering substances from the home is that some recovering addicts will tell you that having it around does not bother them. If you hear this from an addict in early recovery, they might believe what they are saying, but it is their addiction talking. The addict is unconsciously doing what is called "leaving the door open" to use in the future by ensuring a guaranteed supply of something to use when they are at your home.

The third reason used for not removing alcohol and drugs is that some people are arrogant about not wanting to change their lifestyle, even at the expense of their addicted loved one. They will continue using mind-altering substances around their home, and in the presence of the addict, as if they are unaware of the addict's challenges.

Last, and probably the most common reason for not eliminating mind-altering substances from the home, is that the homeowner or someone else in the home also has an untreated addiction problem. Expecting a person to recover from addiction while living with another practicing addict is preposterous. The addict's chance of recovery under these conditions will be almost zero.

## Events You Host

Many events people host, both inside and outside of their homes, involve the use of alcohol, and in some instances, marijuana or other drugs. Even if they have made their home otherwise alcohol and drug-free for the addict, people will feel obligated to make it available at special events they are hosting. Backyard barbeques, graduations, watching sporting events on TV with buddies, and wedding receptions are all good examples of these types of events. Sometimes people have been hosting annual events for years.

All the excuses for not removing substances from the home apply to these special events. However, when you bring people from outside the immediate family into the equation, it causes you to introduce another excuse for not taking prudent action. The excuse may go something like this, "What will they think of us if we are not providing alcoholic beverages at the event? If we do not provide it, they might think we have addiction issues in our family. Maybe they will think we are too cheap to supply the booze." This excuse is grounded in misguided, vanity-based thinking.

Here are some examples of proven, effective actions people take to deal with the issue of having mind-altering substances at special events:

- Hold the events early in the day, for example, a pancake breakfast,

- Host the events outside of your home at a restaurant or other venue that does not serve alcoholic beverages, and

- If the addict is active in recovery and will agree to it, let people know the event will be alcohol and drug-free. If they ask why, tell them you have a person recovering from addiction in the family and that you are creating a supportive environment for them.

So much of what we do in relation to hosting events is habitual. Our behavior is dictated to us by the media and by the actions of others around us. This is particularly true when it comes to serving alcoholic beverages.

You should ask yourself the question, which is a variation on the guiding principle provided under Responsibility #2, "Do I want the addict to get better or do I want these people to like me?" You need to challenge yourself with this thought. If people look down on you or disassociate with you because you are hosting an event without alcohol or drugs, these are likely pretty thin relationships. In addition, you might be surprised at how many of these people have a loved one in their family that they should be doing the same thing for — you might be an inspiration!

## Activities Outside Your Home

There are many events, which are hosted by other people, where alcoholic beverages, and even drugs, might be provided. Examples of these are weddings, graduation parties, birthday parties, and dinner engagements. Unlike events you host, you cannot control what they serve, but this does not mean that you are powerless in this area.

If you have a person in your home who is struggling with addiction, who would normally attend these outside events with you, you have some very good options for supportive actions to take.

- Do not attend the event. For the benefit of the addict, you can simply decline the invitation and make up a viable reason for not attending.

- Plan to attend the event, but only stay for a short period. As an example, for weddings you can attend the ceremony, but not the reception.

- Plan another activity with the addict at the same time as the other event.

Some of this might sound a bit covert and dishonest. However, it is not if you consider that you are trying to help someone with a serious physical and psychological condition. Additionally, keep in mind what many addicts, and their families, are told in recovery circles — "People are not that focused on what you do, or do not do!" The people who are inviting you to the event are probably not thinking about you fifteen seconds after you let them know you will not be attending (or after you leave early). Our self-importance tells us they are thinking otherwise.

## Being Drunk or "High" Around the Addict

You can eliminate the presence and use of alcohol and drugs on a day-to-day basis in your home, and deal with the special events, but you can still make the mistake of being drunk or "high" around the addict. Doing this creates two issues — smelling like it and behaving as if you have used a substance. If the addict knows you, as you know them, they can tell when you are under the influence.

Maintaining your sobriety around the addict is important because it communicates the message that you do not have to "get high" to enjoy life. If you have trouble staying "straight" in front of the addict, you should review the reasons/excuses that were presented earlier in this section.

## Unnecessary Stress

Throughout the book, it has been advanced that the addict must suffer the consequences of their addictive behavior. To this end, it has been recommended that you do not enable the addict's poor behavior and that you set boundaries in areas that you control. The stress that the addict feels, as they experience the negative impact of their addictive behavior, is not the subject of this action step. Unnecessary stress is caused by you being unreasonable around the addict and creating stress that is not directly related to the addiction. Bluntly, when you are not being a very nice person.

Depending on your personal communication style, and how you deal with people, this action step could represent one of the greatest challenges to you out of anything described in this book. If you are opinionated, demanding, aggressive, over-emotional, or controlling, you need to discontinue this type of behavior. Dysfunctional behavior of this type, on your part, will only move the addict away from recovery and toward their coping mechanism — the alcohol or drugs.

As described in Responsibility #2, you should strive to achieve a loving, compassionate, calm, and patient relationship with the addict; a relationship without anger, judgment, or blame and with a willingness to listen. This does not mean you need to behave around the addict in an overly cautious manner. The goal should be normal give-and-take with the addict, governed by the boundaries you have established.

## Responsibility #6

### Conduct a formal intervention with the addict if you believe it is appropriate.

Conducting an intervention is an action that can be very effective for helping an addict decide to pursue treatment. The issue with conducting an intervention is when, and if, to do it.

An intervention is a carefully planned group session involving the addict and the addict's loved ones. As a part of this intervention, each person expresses their love and describes how the addict's negative behavior has affected their relationship. Along with this, each person expresses their desire to have the addict pursue treatment, then lets them know what the change in their relationship will be if they do not get into recovery. Often this comes in the form of telling the addict that they will no longer be a part of the addict's life if they continue their current path.

Normally, as part of an intervention, treatment has been prearranged and the addict is asked to immediately take up the group's offer for the treatment. Additionally, engaging a professional to help organize and execute the intervention is the best way to make it successful. Having a third party involved in planning and facilitating the actual intervention helps convey the seriousness of the activity to the participants and the addict.

There is no standard guideline for when it is appropriate to conduct an intervention. As a general rule, if you are attempting the actions suggested in this book or by your support groups, and the addict's situation continues to deteriorate, you should conduct an intervention. Early intervention, rather than waiting until the addict's situation becomes dismal, is prudent.

One of the big errors people make with an intervention is viewing it as a quick fix to the problem. If an addict goes into treatment because of an intervention, but comes out of treatment into an environment that is enabling, without boundaries, and missing all the other elements of effective recovery support, the addict's chances of long-term recovery will be slim. If you have already established a recovery relationship with the addict and are fulfilling other recovery support responsibilities, an intervention is a natural extension of what they have already been experiencing with you.

There is no assurance an intervention will cause a person to enter treatment. Further, there is no guarantee that getting them into treatment will result in them pursuing an active program of recovery. However, even if the addict does not accept the group's offer of treatment, there are still some significant benefits to conducting the intervention. These include an overall group awareness of the importance of being unified about how to help the addict, a group understanding of setting boundaries and establishing consequences, and having the knowledge you are doing everything you can to facilitate recovery.

### Responsibility #7
### Secure your personal property and other assets from abuse by the addict.

One of the last things people think about when they enter the process of trying to help an addict is protecting their home, its contents, and other personal property against acts of theft or other abuse by the addict. The first time many people act in this regard is when something happens that triggers distrust in the addict. Perhaps you notice cash or other valuables missing from your home.

The first reason that people do not act to protect their property is that they cannot imagine the person they love, the person they are trying to help, doing this to them. The reaction by most people to stealing, or other property related abuse by the addict, is some combination of denial, insult, and astonishment. They had not even considered protecting their personal property and other assets from abuse.

Another reason people do not protect their personal property is that they cannot see how it is going to help the addict. At a very basic level, protecting your property takes away some possibilities for the addict to get into trouble. Also, dealing with theft and other issues can be very time consuming for you, and can take you away from other recovery support activities that are far more valuable.

Remember, as the disease progresses the substance becomes the number one priority in the addict's life. Loving you and stealing from you to get money for alcohol or drugs are completely different subjects to them.

The purpose of this section of STOP is to provide insight into the types of property that can be the target of an addict and to provide a suggested strategy for handling several common situations that arise. To start, here are several examples of property that can become the target of theft or abuse by someone struggling with addiction:

## Property Examples

- Homes and other real estate
- Business assets and lines of credit
- Investments
- Personal checks
- Credit cards
- Cash
- Passwords (bank accounts/shopping sites)
- Identity (social security numbers and other ID)
- Automobiles, motorcycles, and boats
- Computers and phones
- Televisions, stereos, and video players
- Video games and cartridges
- Cameras
- Jewelry
- Firearms
- Sterling silver and gold items
- Collections of coins and stamps
- Sporting equipment

- Clothing
- Power tools
- Art
- Furniture
- Liquor and prescription medicines

The actions that you will need to take to protect a specific property item will be dependent on the characteristics of that property.

## Joint Ownership

When there are two or more people who have a legal claim to the property, it presents a significant risk to the non-addicted property owners. This is true because, without restrictions, the addict will have open access to the property.

The most common joint ownership situations are in marriage and business. In the case of marriage, a spouse who is addicted and gets into a financial bind can empty the joint checking, savings, and investment accounts with relative ease. Looking at a joint business arrangement, the addict has many avenues to put the business in jeopardy.

What a person must do if they believe their joint property is at risk, is speak to an attorney about what actions they should take to secure their share of the property and to protect it from abuse. Unfortunately, there are not many opportunities to set effective boundaries in joint property situations, so legal changes to the status of the assets are usually the only option.

As a note, going to see an attorney is a difficult action for many people to take. They feel as if they are going behind the addict's back, the addict will feel deceived, and this will drive the addict deeper into their addiction. Keep in mind the misguided beliefs presented earlier in the book and try to be confident about the need to act if you have joint assets at risk.

### Entrusted Property

Entrusted property is property that you own and loan to someone for use. Depending on the laws in your area, and the type of item that was entrusted, the owner can be held liable for illegal acts committed by the person using the property. Automobiles, motorcycles, boats, and guns are good examples of property that can be entrusted and then misappropriated.

The most common example of this type of property abuse, which comes up in family support groups, is a young person, struggling with addiction, who is driving a car that is titled and insured by the parents. Destroying the vehicle and hurting themselves, or others, are all real possibilities in the hands of an addict. Depending on the laws where you live, the parents can be held accountable legally and financially for whatever mishap occurs with the vehicle.

Continuing with the example of the entrusted vehicle, to protect against this type of situation from occurring, people can take a variety of actions. These include putting the car in the addict's name and requiring them to pay their insurance or setting a boundary and then taking the car away if there is any evidence of driving under the influence.

Your circumstances with the entrusted property will dictate the action that is most appropriate. This is another area where consulting an attorney can be a good idea.

### Property Subject to Identity Theft and Fraud

Property falling into this category represents items that can be stolen from you and then used to access cash or cash equivalents. Personal checks, credit cards, social security numbers, and passwords to computers, bank accounts, and shopping sites are included in this category. The challenge of having these items stolen from you, for example by a person living in your home, is that the theft can go undetected for a long period. In that time, the addict can do some serious damage to your personal affairs.

Concerning items like checks and credit cards, you need to be conscious about the whereabouts of these items and not make it easy for someone to steal them. Relative to passwords, which would provide access to computers, bank accounts, and shopping sites, you need to change these often and keep any record of the passwords in a very secure spot. If you have a home safe, that would be an ideal place to store them.

## Valuable Household Items

The fourth category of property includes any of the items on the example property list that can be stolen from your home and sold for cash. All of the items on the list have four distinguishing characteristics — value, size, the frequency of use, and portability. The items that would be good targets are those that have high value, are small, infrequently used, and portable; particularly items that you might not notice missing until long after they have been taken.

Examples of small, valuable items that might be used infrequently and are portable include jewelry, cameras, coin collections, and firearms. Also falling into this group is liquor and prescription medicines, which the addict can "skim" from your supply a little at a time and use it for themselves or sell it. To protect the high probability items from theft, a home safe or safety deposit box at a bank is recommended.

Considering all the property you own, regardless of the type, it would be prudent to set boundaries with the addict that cover theft or abuse in any form. As previously illustrated, there are numerous possibilities for actions you can take, but requiring someone to move out of your home or calling the police should not be discounted as possibilities.

The starting point for determining which actions you might take to protect your property is to perform a comprehensive inventory of everything you own. This would include all of the items illustrated in the sample property list.

### Responsibility #8

**Continue to perform your responsibilities whether or not the addict is in recovery.**

As you have learned, recovery from addiction is a process which involves initial treatment followed by long-term maintenance. When the person has acquired the new tools of recovery, they can live free from the burden of the addiction and the accompanying chaotic and unhealthy lifestyle. Continuing this new lifestyle is dependent on the addict maintaining their perspective on recovery and keeping a good frame-of-mind. When relapse occurs, it is because the addict has lost touch with the principles of recovery and has drifted back to their old ways of thinking and behaving.

Like the addict, you must view your addiction support responsibilities as being a long-term undertaking. If you are not diligent about operating with the new tools provided to you in this book, and by your support groups, it is possible for you to revert back to your old thinking and behaviors as well. In other words, it is possible for you to relapse. You should take the view that you and the addict are both participating in a long-term process of change.

One of the great rewards people supporting an addict find is that their own lives have also improved significantly. Why? Because the tools you acquire in the process of helping the addict are effective in all aspects of your life. Not enabling bad behavior in others, setting boundaries, and taking similar actions are very effective in all relationships. Just the process of questioning some beliefs that you have held throughout your life can be a real eye-opener.

\*\*\*\*\*\*\*\*\*\*

# Bibliography *

- Abraham J. Twerski, M.D. - Addictive Thinking - Hazelden Publishing - 1997

- Craig Nakken - The Addictive Personality - Hazelden Publishing - 1996

- Michael Kuhar Ph.D. - The Addicted Brain - FT Press - 2015

- James Robert Milam and Katherine Ketcham - Under the Influence - Bantam - 1983

- Jim MacLaine - When Someone You Love is Addicted to Alcohol or Drugs - Bantam - 2001

- Griffith Edwards - Alcohol: The World's Favorite Drug - Thomas Dunne Books - 2002

- Terrence T. Gorski and Merlene Miller - Staying Sober - Independence Press - 1986

- Arnold M. Washton - Willpower's Not Enough - William Morrow Paperbacks - 1990

- Allen Berger Ph.D. - 12 Smart Things to Do When the Booze and Drugs Are Gone - Hazelden Publishing - 2010

- Dick Schaeffer - Choices & Consequences - Hazelden Publishing - 1998

- Allison Bottke - Setting Boundaries with Your Adult Children - Harvest House Publishers - 2008

# Bibliography *
## (Continued)

- Karen Casey - Let Go Now - Embracing Detachment - Conari Press - 2010

- Angelyn Miller, MA - The Enabler - Wheatmark - 2011

- Dr. David Curry - First Aid for Enablers - Rescue Mission - 2011

- Jeff Jay and Debra Jay - Love First - Hazelden Publishing - 2008

- Melody Beattie - Codependent No More - Hazelden Publishing - 1986

- William L. White - Slaying the Dragon - Chestnut Health Systems - 1998

- Anonymous - Alcoholics Anonymous - AA World Services - 2008

- Anonymous - How Al-Anon Works - Al-Anon Family Groups - 2014

- William D. Silkworth - "Alcoholism as a Manifestation of Allergy" - Central Park West Medical Record - 1937

- Dale Mitchel - Silkworth: The Little Doctor Who Loved Drunks - Hazelden - 2002

- Jane Adams - When Our Grown Kids Disappoint Us - Free Press - 2004

# Bibliography *
## (Continued)

- Sally and David B. - Our Children Are Alcoholics - Islewest - 1997

- David Gust, Sheila Walker, and Jon Daily - How to Help Your Child Become Drug Free - Self-Published - FishLine Print Specialists - 2006

- Dr. Frank Lawlis - Not My Child - Hay House, Inc. - 2014

- Jerome Levin - Introduction to Alcoholism Counseling - Taylor & Francis - 1990

- Charles Rubin - Don't Let Your Kids Kill You - New Century Publishers - 2007

- Joel Young and Christine Adamec - When Your Adult Child Breaks Your Heart - Lyons Press - 2015

* Organized by subject matter

## About the Author

Glenn Rader is an accomplished business professional and writer who turned his talents to helping people who are addicted to alcohol and drugs. His specific area of interest is providing guidance to family members and friends who are trying to help a loved one with a substance abuse issue.

Through Mr. Rader's direct experience working with families and friends of addicts at a major addiction treatment center, he developed first-hand knowledge of the actions that people have taken trying to help an addict, both the successes and the failures. This knowledge, combined with his personal success with recovery from alcohol and drug addiction, and research in the subject area, led to the writing of this groundbreaking book — STOP.

Maze Publishing

# Personal Notes

Made in the USA
Middletown, DE
03 September 2021

47531931R00062